NEVER TRY TO OUTSWIM A BEAR

FIONA CURRAN

WRECKING BALL PRESS

Publications:

At Core was published in Magma No 40

Corporation Roses and ***Fallow*** were published in Loose Muse: An Anthology of New Writing by Women, Spring 2012

The Falling Man was published in Ekphrastia Gone Wild, Poems inspired by Art

The Lover Leaves the Bedroom and ***Not/Almost Still Life*** was published in Issue 10 of South Bank Poetry

Goal was published in Under the Radar, Issue 9

Tobacco Nests, About Mrs Box, Never Try to Outswim a Bear, Involute Piano, & ***The Veneer*** were all published in The Wolf, Issues 13, 16, 20, 29 & The Wolf: A Decade 2002 - 2012

360 Degrees and ***Post*** were published by Bare Hands, online, Issue 11

Empties: Found Items: An Islington Romance was produced as part of the Cursive Script Podcast, online, Issue 2

The Language of Flowers, Daffodils, Lilies and The Bridal Bouquet were published by Textsound, online, Issue 16

The Object of Affection was recorded by Alex Kolkowski for Phonographies, and performed on Resonance FM

Earthed was used in the making of the Earthed series by the film collective NoMoneyInThis, 2014

NEVER TRY TO OUTSWIM A BEAR
FIONA CURRAN

ISBN 978-1-903110-74-4

First published in this edition 2020 by Wrecking Ball Press.

Cover design: humandesign.co.uk

LOTTERY FUNDED
Supported using public funding by
ARTS COUNCIL ENGLAND

For the Reivers

CONTENT

At La Ferté 11
Piano 12
Study For Six Miniatures 13
Earthed 15
The Language Of Flowers 17
Daffodils, Newport, South Wales 18
Lilies 19
The Bridal Bouquet 20
Crown 21
The Veneer 22
Blunt Instrument 24
Bull 26
Old Bear 27
Never Try To Outswim A Bear 28
Salt Draft 30
Walker 32
Travels Without My Aunt
- I. St Ives 33
- II. Arran 34
- III. Roma 35
- IV. Home 36
- V. Rome 37
- VI. On Tour 38
- VII. Krakow 39
- VIII. Hamburg 40
- IX. Roma 41
- X. Paris 42
- XI. Galicia 43
- XII. Hío 44
- XIII. Liméns 45
- XIV. Florence 46

XV. Carlisle 47
All About My Mother 48
The Coat 50
The Scientist Series
I. Basic Experiment 1: Fractional Distillation 52
II. Gf 54
III. The Scientist Avoids 55
IV. The Wave 56
V. Kahlo Syndrome 57
VI. The Frantic Heart 58
VII. The Blackest Part 60
VIII. Eureka 61
IX. Remains 62
The Object Of Affection 63
About Mrs Box 65
Almost/Not Still Life 66
Involute 67
Rider 68
R.A.F. Crewman's Horror At Paper Plane Deficit 69
Goal 70
Doppelgänger 71
Post 72
360° 73
The Lover Leaves the Bedroom Never to Return 74
Fallow 75
At Core 76
The Falling Man 77
Empties: Found Items: An Islington Romance 78
Corporation Roses 79
Tobacco Nests 80
Pellet 81

AT LA FERTÉ

After a painting by Richard Parkes Bonington

You are not waiting, despite what they say
It is the finest vantage point in the bay
But you are not watching.

The red coat is not just for being seen
And it does not make you the harlot
That the local gossips claim.

And the path that scythes the scrub
Is not always retraced, against the expectations
On your old fancies' face.

Waves break; ship after foreign ship
Dot the view; the beloved is not below decks
She sees through

While the wind whips her cheeks into a flare,
Fair hair smoking; yet he sails on, oblivious, mapping
A body greater than her own.

PIANO

The girl sits. The word Mother will eventually swallow her,
But not today, scales pouring from those showgirl fingers
Practice means escape, if she does not side step the upright
In the name of him and him and him, fall for a man too poor
To rent a piano in.

But she does just that and though she still sings,
Her fingers prize only blind pay packets out of drunken pockets,
Her own songs never surface again once the second child is born.

It took a war to liberate and a single day to reign back in,
Until piecemeal all ideals were confined to the shelf of the self,
Put away like good china, so high that dusting became another chore.
Rationed so long you did without yourself.

And so I did not sit, Sunday scrubbed beneath the boom of tingling strings,
Coal flaming my face, while you sang Mahler or thundered out hymns,
But you are extant in my mind with added scratches and too much time,
The sensual stolen by the cylinder.

My imagination locks at the thought of Mother Mary's secrets,
A woman eclipsed, self-scarred by all the usual terrors.
Fermata.   What do I know? She says, laughing,
Inverting the score of her inner life, she begins appassionato.

STUDY FOR SIX MINIATURES

Tasting Failure
At first it is bitter,
Then little by little
Like Greek coffee
Shown sugar
It becomes possible.

The Terrain
No Hero and Leander we,
The Thames and all her bridges
Cannot connect those kisses
And old Neptune sighs
And twists the bracelet on his wrist.

Vignette
The spark arcs between us.
The oils reflect
The plumpness of lips,
The pulse that folds with the wrist,
Tightening sinew, muscle, bone.
Gordian to the beholder.

The Banks
Not quite young Leander
Tolling to his death
And old lovers crowd the banks
Stiff with symbolism.
Determined, you wade through,
I raise the promised golden robe.

Tableau

Hellespont on a choppy night,
Hands cupped you call against the bore,
Tireless Charon is nowhere in sight.
I look on, backlit from the door
Knowing you'll have to swim for it.

Shell

In his deaf ear
The white noise of anticipation
And faintly, skirting the scar
Hero's cries. She knows all too well
Her love is no life raft.
Leander's body pounds the shore.

EARTHED

Goosebumps stand like ranges
Which frame this ruin.
Once the head of an Easter Island idol,
The granite skin sags,
Like a soft country.
The measles jab, a lunar crater.
The valley of the breastbone
Emphasized in the dusk light
Houses a thinking man's folly.

See she contemplates the final grounding
Of the self in the continent of the body.
The Plateau of the back,
In every freckle, the promise of Eden
A daisy down blanket thrown over the skin
In warmer climes.

Now dilapidated, owner-occupied
The low land bracken is galvanized by thunder,
The weather front of a Michel rolls unashamedly over
that which could only belong
To Rembrandt, to Kollwitz.

Never mind, with restless hands
I have come down to earth at last,
And queued to enter what the sages say
Is the vestige of a temple.
But it isn't easy
When you've spent so long in flight
To be earthed
Struggling across the polar landscape,
Blood as slow as condensation
And louring just over there, there -
The sharp squall before
The final transformation.

THE LANGUAGE OF FLOWERS

Arrangement

With yellow carnations he declared; we are dead they said.
Even now, my sister in her engagement weeds,
Her horrified face looking up from the dictionary
Saying, "this cannot be right", radiating pity.
And on a far away mantle, the clock quartered,
Striking another sliver of hope from my heart.

Calling Card

What to do, when another floral tribute,
Opulent, all tuberose and costly exotics
Sent no doubt by that filthy flirt Osborne,
Grandiose, yet smelling of the mills,
Sits in the drawing room,
While my devoted ranunculus languish in the hall?
Is it worth I wonder even leaving my card?
Must I love her even more extravagantly?

Flower Girl

There's no romance sir
In a cress-stuffed piss pot under the bed,
While the dawn breaks itself over my weary back again.
Weeds and watercress for the likes of us,
Some maid of all work tricked to wed
By a primrose presented by a coal man.

DAFFODILS, NEWPORT, SOUTH WALES

Yes I know, but what can you do?
There were great teardrop swathes of them.
Even under a black March sky
They were buttery, cheerful, bedded in banks
And the dead had not yet reached up
To eat them.

I have in my head sacrilegious picking,
But can't be sure and what remains
Is yellow, the storm clouds and you
Leather jacket, Cuban heels,
Your black curls dancing.
A rough hillside for a seduction, Andy,
But we were young and poor
And really anywhere will do
To lock lips and love, relieve the gloom.
Your implausibly large hands roaming.

LILIES

Splendid. A symphonic smell
Sucking the air from the whole room
As they have sucked horror from the earth
Filtering the decay of our bodies' putrefaction.
It is a hard job and some corruption remains,
Catching the back of the throat
So we taste the smell,
Yet we give the blooms over and over again.

Because deep in one strand of our DNA
Where Xenoturbella lurks,
We recognize the earthy delight of what is rotting.
At a molecular level we are signaled,
Come to the soil again
Feel blindly towards the scent of the full-stop.

THE BRIDAL BOUQUET

For Anna Collin and Ben Jones, on this, their wedding day,
28th April 2012

"I have gathered a posy of other men's flowers
and nothing but the thread that binds them is my own"
John Bartlett

Yes, once. But not any more,
No need of dandelion clocks and floating wishes
The capricious carnation has been banished
And in its place, in April, blooms the cactus flower.

Humble. But it needs to be tough in this world
If it wants to endure. And in a nod to the Holly,
It spreads it roots wide and drinks love from the landscape.
You are its fertile grassy plane.

There is a place in the posy for Jasmine,
The thoughtful Pansy, even Narcissus shall have its day,
But you must always return to the Queen of the Night
Her sly secret open for only hours
Yet everything you need to know of love is witnessed in her flowers.

The reservoir of kindness, the table of compassion,
Rude affection, all must be maintained. So kiss often,
A kiss never happens by accident.

CROWN

The new hairdresser informs me,
From the back it runs

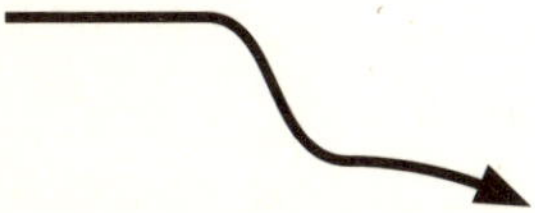

And from the front

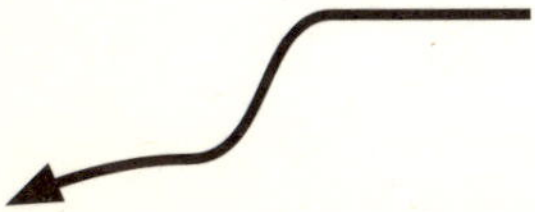

My twin crowns in rebellion.

I imagine this happened in the womb,
Pressed down against my Mother's pelvis,
Thumb sucking, in the best yoga pose I will ever manage
While my black locks licked and formed
And I, second in line, anointed twice, was born
And the world welcomed me.

My hair uncontrolled is still apt to riot,
Inside and out, the head must be governed
But at least the day tiara covers
The scars that rainy day ache,
The blunt stub of my horns.

THE VENEER

The snarl escaped, broad and hot,
No amount of education
Could erase the visceral reaction
To a thief, all thumbs
Fingering my designer tote,
Obvious. A windmill tilting for a fix.
The name I called her was the worst name,
The one women must reclaim
Before it is too late.
The vile slander scared her off,
She went her desperate way
And we returned wine-watered
To bourgeois art.

But later this me,
The thinly disguised she,
Is curled up on the battered
Three-piece suite of the mind,
Sipping a breezer, smoking a fag,
Slipper bobbing.
'See', (she's been thinking on)
'You've nothing to fear when you are me',
Except me of course.
Proper hardcore underneath
The gene pool rippling still,
Ancestral DNA poking through
And the fresh kill spitting.

The coarse hand of the Southern Ape,
Or Nietzsche's creature after that,
Feels the snug fit of the club.

BLUNT INSTRUMENT

The women of the house awake
And the shrew more awake than ever,
Abandoned by the killer kitten
Eviscerated, heart fit to explode.
So, no way back,
We could leave it to the owl and the moon
But that would be beyond cruel,
The job of its death falls to me.

I have not killed since childhood spiders
And now I must be swift, merciful and kill.
I cover with burnt leaves,
Conceal the eye, its fearful pain,
Deliver the blow but no fatality,
The shrew's breath fills the universe
An inhalation as sharp as my own.
Disgusted by my cowardice, my lack of will,
Twice more the hammer, the beast is dead.

I feel dizzy with death momentarily, revolted.
Before moving the shrew to its place of decomposition,
(How can I say rest?) I take a deep luxurious breath,
Look up at the bracken hills
A Jacque landscape come to life.
I have killed properly for the first time,
I see Ted raise his gun on his beloved dog,
TP, the knife and the shrieking sow,
Nurses hovering over my Mother's head.

I move the tiny enormity to the herb garden
Let it become bone amongst mint and yarrow.
The hammer pulls at my shoulder,
The implement run through December dew
Before returning it innocent, to the shelf.

BULL

Bull, who had they torn you from?
Mighty bellow, catching the corners of the house,
Making the landscape reverberate
And the birds momentarily silent.

Watch out for the bull they said,
"Proud Farmer and his Prize Bull".
You belong to the 18th Century School,
Even with your head twisted towards us,
Character presumptuous,
You have the massive flatness of a map,
Squareness of flank, a low-slung bulk;
The weight is solid though, muscle rolling
Through thighs to ribs and neck
As you swell and trot towards us.

There is no need to snort Hell,
You know the smell of fear.
No labyrinth between us and the stile
We retreat behind the hawthorn,
Stand safely eye-to-eye.
You are a big blonde brute, handsome,
With curls and cowlicks, the tousled hair
Of a Beau Brummel dandy.
We draw no swords but simply stare.
And out of the frame the milkmaid stands
Wondering how she will cross the field
This morning.

OLD BEAR

Winter reigns,
Driving the bear deeper into the den,
She has brushed the last guilty leaves aside
And ball-like waits for peace to strike.

Sometimes, like a mother, asleep with eyes wide
She appears comprehending,
But she has drawn down to the nub
And easy prey amble through dreams.

Suspended, no blastocyst preserved in time
She feels each season more passionately,
Desires no society but that of ticks,
Her fur will baffle all comers until spring
When she and territory stand afresh.

When she comes forth, svelte for a bear
Eyes bleary, womb aghast,
She wonders how she comes to be here again
Among twitching birds, sun singing to the earth,
But here she is, scratching,
Another year away from birth.

NEVER TRY TO OUTSWIM A BEAR

Not merely a matter of danger, but of common courtesy. You will "show him up" and if he's a northern bear he'll be reduced in the eyes of his fellow bears to something approaching a sloth.

Similarly, the washing of teddy must be undertaken when the bear least expects it. He must be plucked from the cot or crib while young Biff is at nursery or you can persuade your little darling that "bear is swimming" and if there's one thing a bear really enjoys, it's being pegged up by his ears.

If, in an unguarded moment, you have pitched a two man tent by the lake, in some idyllic untouched wilderness, do not expect the male, emerging from his morning constitutional, to wipe his feet before rummaging through the "snack bag" or eating your fiancée. By the way, he will not nibble her, or necessarily be happy with just an arm.

Is said bear in the swimming pool? If so you'll find him tough to share lanes with and should you be so foolish as to try backstroke, all that random splashing may make him think he's on to the big one, because he can't remember when he last saw a salmon that slow and fat.

Capsized? White river rafting, holiday ferry or on the ice flow, anyway, a long way from a "controlled environment" and that thing you can smell, part Bovril, part death, is the aforesaid mentioned bear's breath. Should you make it ashore before Mr. Bear, I would advise you not to gloat, but to run. Run like Jessie Owens, run like twenty years of training have come to this, it's the moment you have waited your whole life for –explode from the blocks, the mind is clear, the medal in sight. Yes!

What play dead? Well you can try a swoon.
Yes, you can try.

SALT DRAFT

For the submariners of K1141 Kursk

Fingers edged with salt, water shin deep but rising. On the blank side of a coded dispatch, you are going to write to her, not waste time pounding out an SOS, delivered only to the deep. God's own navy crewed by angels wouldn't be able to save you now.

Last cigarettes lit. A hundred theories float as deflated and useless as the lifejackets. You sweat and freeze at once, who would believe it? Fingers strain to curl, pen clamped above damp paper, a red lamp lit by a last light giving no heat. In the eddy of the flood you see her, the internal drift presents your beloved bride, a girl not yet disabused of the notion that you are her world and all that's in it. Now is the time for illusions and here she comes running down the gangplank, arms outstretched to the viewfinder. Rewind. Recorded the day your loved ones came to admire their only rival, the darling of the fleet, our boys steel sweetheart, unsinkable by design, now all hands down and you with her.

All warmth has begun its withdrawal into the brick centre of the body, last coals in the chest; you must get on, no time this time for crossing out, corrections or attempted perfection. So you tell her, *Darling we're finished, we're sinking.* You try reassurance, it whistles round the hull of your heart, but you tell her to go on as best she can and you tell her that you love her. You pour your soul into the last ink kiss.

Silt. Thigh high the water has a grainy feel, an hourglass quality. You flatten the letter in the cipher bag; press it to your chest. Sealed in nicely, like yourself, this lonely testimony won't float away. Done. Certain you have done all you can with words, eventually all will surface.

A Hail Mary dies in your throat. Some fool is singing a shanty in the dark. To your left, terrible laugher, expelling doubt. You listen, deciding not to struggle when the water comes for your lungs via nose and mouth, which is now.

WALKER

After Lee Marvin

No quarter, point blank.
The Marine marches up to death,
Brisk, going at a lick,
He wouldn't break his stride
For the devil himself.
The subliminal snarl, while feet drum
Baby, baby, where did our love go?
Walker. He has no time for prisoners.
He threw me to the ground,
I smacked him right back;
We were both just about satisfied with that.

Postcard I: St Ives

TRAVELS
WITHOUT
MY AUNT

Dearest –

A strip of yellow, then blue, then blue,
then sun, cartwheel upended, yellow
again. A tricolour of happiness, above it
all the haze, evaporated disappointment,
work and all its dominions gone vague in
the heat.

All the clichés of course true, buckets
and sand make children of men, all
woman Nereids; kids feed the gulls with
what falls from their mouths; sun cream,
ice cream and surf conspire to wash
away the every day. Between our toes
the grit that makes the pearl.

WYWH

To
You,
Top Floor Flat,
Main, Main, Road
Concrete-Under-Lime
Landlocked, England

Postcard II: Arran

Darling –

Lots of walking. But little clear thought.
The moon slowly skirts the island. A
lours and says we are bound to see his
stag in the morning. Another dumb
creature endures this relentless rain.

So quiet that the thirup of birds wings is
startling. Only you could do more to
wreck this reverie.

WYWH

To
You,
41st Floor, Vanity Tower,
Sun-On-Steel
Thames to the Left
The City, Always.

Postcard III: Roma

Dear Heart –

Rome of course reminds me of you. It's the stone pines Guido (on which the gods stepped to keep their feet off the grubby populace), they grew and grew and when it all got too much, they laid their heads down exhausted, just like you.

Still, a good spot from which to gaze on the mortal beauties, the coconut cookie nipples of yet another goddess, you will end up pledging yourself to, it's inevitable.
All those promises Guido.
Love is exhausting, isn't it?

Yours, anyway,
F x

To
Me,
Villa Agrodolce,
Via de Ponziano
Trastevere, Roma

Postcard IV: Home

Pappy,

Home at last. To the right Hungerford Bridge, a wind harp singing soprano.

A gentle spell cast at every Rubicon crossing, by my husband, London, whom I still love. Occasionally we consider divorce, but never simultaneously. And he turns a blind eye to my thing with you, old Father Thames. Shall I walk all over you? My toenails, London bus red, your lacquered geisha.

As your moist palm trailing knotweed, travels swiftly up my leg, I drift into your unmade tidal bed. Home at last.

x F

To
Old Father Thames,
Trewsbury Mead,
Gloucestershire,
ST980994

Postcard V: Rome

Dear Me,

Honeysuckle scent floods like a woman
down the embankment walls, delicate
Chantilly desserts await, Frascati
vaporizes on the breath and in a shallow
vestibule between the ladies and the
restaurant floor, a voluptuous woman
and a lover of the Roman School, are
caught.

It is all surface. It is a beautiful kiss. The
waiter has waited; an opportunist who
struck at my lips with sheer nerve; my
hazel eyes, which mirror his, it turned
out, were worth the risk.

And I pressed my hand to his heart, and
the ending, the ending, oh! It was as gentle as
an expiring dente de leone.

F x

To
Me,
The Memory Bank,
Villa Agrodolce,
Via de Ponziano
Trastevere,
Roma

Postcard VI: On Tour

Mikhail,

Scorching. Zen in the legs, the grit under
the wheels crackles like vinyl – a long,
long player. It plays almost as long as
these banks, where crow sentinels, hot
and bored, stand guard on post after
post, disconsolate. Hunching. Their blue-
black mantle echoes your sad back as
you turned from me at Gare du Nord.
Your footsteps slap, pace my mind long
after you had left. The too many
miles between us – a protracted zoom.
A space crow's view of the universe.

Now it's nothing but pylons promising
death and the banks, the banks.

x F

To
M.B.
A Suburb,
Qui se soucie où
Paris,
Yes Paris
France.

Postcard VII: Krakow

Dear Ludo,

You see, she is seated, sleeves like spitting plums reveal a deep red flesh: the knotting of arteries over golden bones beneath. And that creature cradled in your arms, beautiful Cecelia, bites. You are unperturbed though, knowing your revenge for his disobedience, the sinking of pin-prick teeth, would be swift– the result, a white winter collar, warmer than all others.

And she looks off to the left at the distant flames of burning cities or burning hearts, while Leo paints and paints and paints. Then Cesare starts off kicking; setting the stoat wriggling and she bursts out laughing.

X

To
Ludo Storza,
Duke of Milan
Court of Milan
Milan,
Milan.

Postcard VIII: Hamburg

Container Heart Lands;
Immigrant Sadness in the
Power House of Europe

To
The 3 Young men in,
FCCU 216319 1
Fleeing, Afloat,
In the Gulf of Aden,
To the gateways of Europe

Postcard IX: Roma

Jep,

Great to see you, AGAIN at another party to end all parties!

I'm very near the epicentre, but not quite near enough, and the alignment of the plates grinds on. So the way forward, via the past, is still obscured. Somewhere in the sediment is the key to you and I, to all of it. A key, flattened, beaten wafer thin, a tray tough enough to toboggan on, down the smooth white past (so many times interrogated), into the black run to the future.

On the horizon stands everything, but as we rush to meet it, it appears to be nothing more significant than a full stop. Damn.

F x

To
Jep Gambardella
Villa Alighieri,
Somewhere near the
Coliseum,
Roma, Forever Roma.

Postcard X: Paris

M,

For God's sake mon ami, not the Verdurins, that stupid, vapid, dizzy, insensitive, vicious, meddling creature and her braggart husband; claiming Elstir was incapable of knowing what to paint until she told him what was worthy of his floral talents. Jasmine! Would she smelled as sweet! She is beyond vulgar; say what you like about Odette (and by God they do), but I'd rather her than that vache. Any day.

So no, I'd rather have an early night. Of course I shall see you in Balbec as usual. I look forward to tea, served by the stubborn Françoise, as always.

X F

To
M.P.
102 Boulevard Haussmann,
75008,
Paris
France

Postcard XI: Galicia

Beloved,

We bathe again and leaving our beautiful
beach, (with water a degree warmer
than death) we headed for lunch – the
central ritual. All Spaniards, of course,
gourmets. After dangling pimentos, we
settle for magnificent sardines, the
delicate pillow white flesh giving way to
muddy hues, a warning to stay away from
this internal rust. Chipirones
basking in onions have the inky quality
of liver. Creamy Pulpo washed down
with local Ribeiro. Finally soft coffee,
which has no effect; then the group
fragments, winds slowly home for the
inevitable siesta.

Tomorrow I will have a sun-warmed
muscatel in a bar full of old men who are
sly.

Xxx F

To
You,
Far away, but near really,
In a small but pretty town
in England.

Postcard XII: Hío

My Heart,

Sol poniente then, the lighthouse
blinking. Black takes on a new
significance in Spain. Today in the
cobblers, the gaps between old leather
shoes suck in the light and extinguish it
innocently; The Virgin in the swirling
alcove at Hío, a dark Dolores, doll-like,
looks down on human sorrow
impassively. We atone by drinking dark
beer served by dark men, and arguing.
On route home, a shining stag beetle on
his hind legs, at battle stations, faces off a
monstrous cat, a huge foe. Then we
sleep in the shuttered, oak-lined house,
midnight blinded; a blackness thick
enough to wear slips off me as I head out
into the dawn to hear the blackbird
chanteuse. On the path a young dead
snake like a question mark.

To
(UNSENT)

Postcard XIII: The Villa: Liméns

M,

A case of all our daughters: sweetened with Chekov, soured with Ibsen. It is impossible to be unhappy on a sunny beach, but in the Spanish shadows, they will have their say, and honesty rages unchecked around the lunch table. Words sharpened against iron experiences. And wielded with intimate knowledge.

But behind each back, one by one they say, “my sister is sensitive, she worries about me”. In other words, there is enough love to go round. It appears in Saint’s day kisses. In platted hair. In breakfast offerings. In love’s insistence. Now I hear their flip-flop feet approaching: they comfort an only child.

D x

To
My Mother,
One of many sisters,
Wherever she and they are now,
A postcard.

Postcard: XIV: Florence

J,

Behind the bossy surfaces of the façades, a splendid (small S) restaurant. Venison in chocolate, nothing unusual. On the next table sit the exquisite: the languid afternoon of love has made them shine; she is a woman who knows her worth and wears it like a good post-modernist. The jewels on her arms, bone and wood and stone, like Italy. Her black curls cut high and heavy. She teases the food on her plate, while he eats with gusto; playing with plaid, Abbarchi shirt, his dark Mazuchelli glasses framing the mouth in motion, another titbit to the full lips. They are the essence of ease and they own everything. They are the greatest works of art in Florence.

x F

To
Jep Gambardella
Villa Alighieri,
Somewhere near the
Coliseum,
Roma,
Ridiculous Roma.

Postcard: XV: Carlisle

You'll remember this Dad. The eels returning, that incredible lustrous band, oil slick black, making its way inland. Thick, rope-like, a yard wide, maybe more. Who knows how long? Back to the firth?

I have it in my head that we watched it together from the disused railway bridge, you know, the one you threw your service revolver off that night, when I was still a baby. But then I seem to be standing in the water, on the other side of the bridge, watching the eels, with my pals behind me; we have been swimming and lazing all day, but no one wants to swim in the band of black, even the boys don't have the nerve. We watch instead, willing something bad to happen.

What I don't get is I don't think I saw this eel migration happen twice, it seems unlikely. Was I with you Dad? If not I doubt I'll ever get to the truth of this *simultaneous view* of the same event. Obviously I've made one of these up, yet they are both so strong in my mind I don't know which to believe. Both films feel conclusive.

Is this the start of it then? Going mad like Mam, or does this happens to everyone? Fuzzy truth. Fragmentation. How would I have known it was the eels if you hadn't told me? Who would have explained it to me? Why did I stand there, up to my waist in the water just watching? Dad, do you know?

XXX Nona

ALL ABOUT MY MOTHER

Lament

Fifteen years on I am ordering a rug.
Am telling a friend it must match this Old Persian affair,
My carpets it seems are revolving around yours,
Bed-bare toes curl on that which once commanded hearth
A rectangle of the old north beneath me.

And all those smoky Sundays are in the wool
Family resigned to the living room,
The rained off constitutional - we play cards instead and argue
Wait for a sunburst.
Then we trample over the red edges and off across the fields

Never reckoning that all that would remain
Was this rug; house gone, children scattered, you dust.
And no other kin to tread what's left into the weave,
No soul rolls up the rug to dance.

Butcher

I used to hate going to that butcher of a Friday,
Standing there while you had your little flirt,
Giggling. A fifty-five year old coquette.
"Is this your sister?" he'd say, tipping his white trilby towards me,
While his sausage fingers sought string to make a love knot,
His eyes promising to slip you a little something extra.

Dirty old bugger and you Mam should have known better.

Now I am at the till and the lad, waving my wine through, says
"Now madam" (they call me madam now)
"Are you quite sure you're eighteen?" I giggle and say I think I will pass,
And take as much joy out of the encounter as I can squeeze
Knowing finally these tokens keep a woman alive
While life stands torn-faced by her side.

Undergarments

A moment of musk as you pass on powdered feet
Then the drama of the toilette, with me acting as lady's maid.
First knickers, sensible, all encompassing (and forgiving)
The corset reinforcement, all straps and hooks and eyes,
For suspenders we chase buttons through the sewing box,
Then the heave-ho of stockings; in the big dance band age
Sister Martha would draw lines up the back of those shapely legs.
In winter a vest, but tonight in the light, just the static-proof slip.
All in white, your innocent maid stands back aghast,
But for that blaze of red lipstick, a standard,
The gauntlet of Joan of Arc.

THE COAT

You are relieving the night shift, unusual for you to do days, but here you are, the dawn stars barely in retreat. It isn't a long journey and you are hardly warm before the country bus, making early morning speed, delivers you into January again. You, who drove ambulances during the war still don't have a civvy license, you make that vigorous internal tut.

You are half way across the duel carriageway, clambering the crash barrier as usual when you see the coat on the southern slip outside the café. You see the coat, the heap, the form under the coat. Martha's coat. Your sister's coat. Your sister's body. And you think you are going to faint, be sick, scream, join her, die on the road first. You have to get across.

All manner of things get in the way of getting to her. Your nephew playing, Ted opening the door, unknowing. Smiling she shows you her dress for the Christmas do. You share the house at the bingo. That big stand up fight; she puts her hand out to pull you up off the sand – you are twenty one and the tail gunner you long to marry awaits and the world belongs to you, Mary. The gulf of grief, wider and longer than this A road. Trucks and trucks and trucks.

Then you are there: green wool, fur collar, and dim though it is, the brooch stands up in the half-light, silver as hoarfrost. Another you, another Mary, can hear voices, feet fast approaching, but you are in the bubble, you reach and reach and reach, it takes so long to touch your sister's shoulder.

Then the hands, but not before you drop to your knees on the tarmac and howl. The shift haul you to your feet, Martha, Martha (?) looks into your eyes, she looks at you full face, she even speaks with her genuine cigarette dimpled voice

Mary! It's Tommy, you know old Tommy, Tommy the tramp! A wagon must of hit him on the slip and I had to cover him, couldn't leave him uncovered see, the police are coming now. Mary! See?

Martha pulls back the edge of the coat, and the still, dead face of Tommy looks out. You begin to breathe again. Poor old Tommy.

The women, still holding you by the elbows walk you into the warmth of the kitchen. Your stockings are torn and your knees are sore and bleeding. Martha wipes away those tears. Out on the tarmac, dawn delivers the day and poor old Tommy stays dead.

THE SCIENTIST SERIES:
GRIEF: EXPERIMENT 1:
FRACTIONAL DISTILLATION

Shall we proceed?

[She lifts an iceberg from the last glaciation on to the bench]

Today, we will be working with grief.

A volatile substance of course.

But if we look beneath the waterline

[The Scientist leans over]

We see, compressed and compacted, the dead.

This one has broken away from the ice-shelf self

And when combined with the undercurrents in which it travels

It will shortly produce

[She lights the Bunsen]

A satisfying gulf stream of grief.

The raw climate, transforming filn

Has frozen and refrozen the sample, and here we see

[She holds up the test tube]

Death is molecular. Sealed inside, the wicked grin

Along with the everyday DNA of those we love.

Applying heat

[She does]

We will see souls spring forth in the thaw

And take to the salt water of creation

[Liquefaction occurs]

Allowing us the living, and they, the dead

To once again intermingle.

Gf

Name: Grief
Symbol: Gf
Atomic weight: 0
Standard state: solid at moment of death
Colour: grey/black
Classification: cellular

Historical Information: Approximately, 3,600,000,000 years. Confirmed by multiple observation, data irrevocable.

Chemistry and Compounds: Note; endless proliferation potential.

Reactions to Grief: to/with, Air; water; halogens; acids; bases and hearts – predictable and entirely mapped.

Isolation: it is not necessary to make grief in a laboratory, as it is readily available worldwide. Extraction is not complex since the method employed depends upon the simple extinction of the signaling and self-sustaining processes contained in any life form. The second step is merely observation of the decay and modification of the molecular remains.

THE SCIENTIST AVOIDS

She would do anything to avoid undertaking the research that awaits.
The contradiction of which, she is well aware.

The results, foregone.
It is the examination of her methodology, the parameters of her inquiry,
Which will lead her on to shaky ground.
And instead of relishing this chance to prove her hypothesis
(Or rest in the knowledge of what is disproved)
She employs methods of distraction, of which she is ashamed
Such as, Sex. Consumerism. Religion. Greed.
Drinking. Holidays. Anything will do.
Nonsense, she chooses nonsense.

THE WAVE

The old man in the van, face flashing in the side mirror,
Thick frame glasses bottle blue grey eyes, wiry hair escaped.
His waving hand, the opening of an enquiry,
Calloused and crêpe; hands which have worked and wrung,
A swallow tattoo, as old as his youth,
Tries to fly the webbing of his fingers.
This flight catches the Scientist unaware
As he waves her bestride her bicycle through.
Avoiding the pedestrians she runs the equation over

$$\frac{\text{memory}}{\text{forgotten detail}} \quad \text{x} \quad \frac{\text{acute observation}}{\text{pain}} \quad = \quad \text{loss}$$

And momentarily she suspects transduction.

KAHLO SYNDROME

Another surgical intrusion Alan
Opened up so many times,
Skin clamped, star-like,
While they rummaged, yes, rummaged around
And found nothing you could name.

Cut and cauterized, grafted,
Muscles grown up the body
Like an ear on the back of a mouse,
They have made you monster.
They tried everything to fill
The hole that follicle made,
Until your back,
Gouged like craters of the moon
Defeated them.
In the end the botch job had to serve –
One more transfusion for luck Mr. Curran
And you'll be on your way.

These doctors, blind to Kahlo Syndrome,
The pain rises from the bed
And makes pictures of its own,
Tethered by dream cords.
The rotting umbilical's hold,
The dear dead and worse to us.

At 3 a.m. the Scientist lies watching the dead revolve
Let me cut these. Let me cut this
She thinks.

THE FRANTIC HEART

Highly reactive or unstable materials are those that have the potential to vigorously polymerize, decompose, condense, or become self-reactive under conditions of shock, pressure, temperature, light, or contact with another material.

Plenty of contact.
The battered heart
Every shade of pink,
Red, purple and grape,
Runs here and there
On its little cartoon legs,
Three great blood tears
Fly from its bloodshot eyes

And the children laugh at the broken heart.

It runs about and runs about,
Looking for a way back
Into the Scientist's body,
But the ribs act as a cattle grid,
Keep it from slipping through
And wrapping the comfort blanket
Of the lungs around it.

God, how it blubs
How it aches!
But it cannot keep up any more
With the crystalline deposits
Once excised by the Scientist,
Which build on her skin
Like hoar frost,
Making her as ghost-like
As those she mourns.

The Heart falls on its bottom
Like a legless tot,
Lies back and looks at the sky
Exhausted. Exhausted.
Keep breathing, it tells the lungs,
Who peep from the chest cavity.

THE BLACKEST PART

Like poor old Henry Jekyll, she cannot tell if it's her, or the compound.
The bloody thing won't separate, so she is stuck with this black heart
Sprouting hair, running wild, terrorizing the lesser organs,
A regular sociopath. While the black ribbons of blood
Run through her aorta like Whitechapel alleys she'll never be safe in.

EUREKA

Dare she acknowledge a breakthrough?
At 5 a.m., the long slow dawn drawn,
The scientist finally concedes
That the dead are everywhere in everything.

Opening the window, wiping away her own breath,
Listening to the optimism of birds,
A lone motorcyclist on an angry Norton
Zips his way to some adventure.
It is her Father delivering dispatches during the war,
She sees him clearly in the rider's back
Dad racing past right now, in the darkest hour,
Over his shoulder he shouts back,
Nona, we're going about our business just like you,
You'll be seeing us, when you least expect it.

Death drops in. In a profile, a blunt pencil,
In a snow storm, with a song on its lips,
Behind aviators, on a full, full plate.
Death drops in wearing a gold dress, laughing,
Asking casually for a light.

So after all this: A Law. Curran's Law states
"The dead are not dead, but present always.
Observable in the minutiae of the daily flux".
- Pain, the inevitable result of such recognition.

REMAINS

The blank page,
The last word,
The winding sheet.

In the mortuary drawer,
In the husk of the body,
The spirit considers its options

1800 degrees for you, vessel,
Then a good grinding
And Ta Ta physical world.

It's sad, for you, yes,
But I am infinite now,
Death no more than a breather,

A long, luxurious stretch.

THE OBJECT OF AFFECTION

..... everything is at sixes and sevens - ladies in love with buggers and buggers in love with womanisers, and the price of coal going up too. Where will it all end?

Lytton Strachey

* * *

Dora Carrington **loves him**, Lytton, the object of her affection and **he adores her**, but it's her husband, Rafe, he **cannot do without**. Rafe's best friend Gerald **is consumed by** Carrington, asks her to elope to Spain, but **she won't leave** the indifferent Lytton. Rafe takes **the first of many** mistresses, **settling eventually** for the generous Frances. The object still **adores the womaniser**, but he too has taken **a young lover, the cupid** Roger. Carrington meanwhile **seeks solace in the arms** of Beacus, the near silent sailor, who **craves her**, but not her body. They all **live together** at Ham Spray, until Roger **abandons** Lytton who is momentarily **broken hearted**. Gertler, the painter who entreated Lytton's help to **capture his beloved** Dora in the first place, **remains enslaved to her**, but she loves only **the object of her affection**.

* * *

So much for the swans, mating once,
The singular heart drumming devotion
Smoke signal confirmation against a pitch sky,
Here is the force that drives the green fuse.
We are the result of all that effort, all that love,

All those circles intersecting at divorce
Began simply; that which couldn't be ignored
Gained momentum, rolled all over their lives
Peopling it with lovers, bastards, wives.

ABOUT MRS BOX

After the painting by Dora Carrington

The body – emblematic, a standard definition,
A low belly begins its swell at the breasts;
Shoulders slope, hands repose without argument,
But beneath the bonnet flushed by evening sun
Everything travels through a face of Flemish exactitude.
Thinking hard, eyes boreholes,
The dry river bed of wrinkles that fringe the lips
Are pursed, deepening the childhood scar
That your mother worried would leave you husbandless.
You were prettier than she thought.
One eye dead, the other stoical
The expression is one we suppose
Of a woman who has lost a dutiful daughter late in life,
Mind weighing not the sorrow but the inconvenience,
Displeasure duly noted, nagging like a lost limb.
The question will be different the moment
She reaches for the poker,
Attends to that which will otherwise be embers.

ALMOST/NOT STILL LIFE

After Brancusi, *Bird in Space 1923*

You vibrate on two axes
Kinesis = muscle memory.

(I can only admire the control)

You are shiny, bold as a Brancusi
I am scratching away
Arrowhead flecked with blood,
The picture jagged,
Because it is hard to see
That which oscillates so tightly.

INVOLUTE

After Hepworth, *Involute 1946*

The stone has spoken, a steady line of force
The form spun out as geometrical perfection.
Excepting the pores which give Involute texture,
Fragility; and the slip
That comes from   time + elements
Your   deliberation/chisel   Barbara.
No sign of the scorch marks to come
Only sly beauty,   a faith in shape.
Only the O.

RIDER

Get me:-

That amp that goes up to 11

And one nubile boy, no make that two,
Have them washed and sent to my room
Resplendent in their birthday suits.

Drugs, no more than usual,
Drink, the same, you know the score,

A grasp of groupies to prey upon,

The smell of fresh cut grass pumped via the air-con,

Failing that, an acolyte of stature,
Rotten say, or John Cooper Clarke, he's a mate
Known for fingering the pulse.

Remember my Lotto. Also

Church wafers, pork scratchings, a photograph of Kant,

Get me heavy duty pornography and a lady boy with baby oil and
Don't forget the dreamcatcher and have the room shamanistically swept.

I don't think there's anything else, except the albino midget to carry my foot stool. But I know getting hold of Larry for a weekday night is a tall order.

R.A.F. CREWMAN'S HORROR AT PAPER PLANE DEFICIT

Byline Fred Curran

"How can anybody leave a Newspaper in the state you do? Look at it!"

It is well read, demolished in fact, but to Dad, R.A.F. running through him like a stick of rock, it is as ruined as one of the cities he bombed during the War.

You, Mother, rightly shrug. Together we look at the photograph on the mantle The uniformed dandy, whites white, crisp indelible creases, cap jaunty. Gorgeous. He who kissed you, whose kisses were worth a lifetime.

"Men and their bloody papers," you mutter, clutching the coupon, waiting for his expression in the square hole, where the division two results should be.

GOAL

Before every goal, the mid-air moment
Stasis, where the team, your team
Are in precisely the wrong position
As the floating ball brings Nike's wrath.
Our inertia is rewarded
By grass spitting dew, studs damp,
Folding legs, heads thrown back
Then bang.
Lofty trepidation suckled by weariness.
Hope lands askew alongside our
So-called defence and relegation,
The ghost of seasons past
Runs his finger along the dusty trophy shelf.

DOPPELGÄNGER

This boy, so much like the other boy,
That I run my hands over my body
Touch here, here, stop.

Down to the blue eyes,
The dirty blue eyes of every cliché.
We look at each other and
We look at each other with surprise.

Three sentences and a magnetic field shared,
While London is torn from the windows,

Books abandoned in laps,
The phenomenon of attraction is considered
And dismissed as ludicrous

Yet still it hangs.

I drop my bag (or could it be myself)
At his feet, out spills one last chance,
But for pleasantry, the gallant thief
Who departs the carriage
Clutching the moment.

POST

The body still thrilled,
The mouth will make any promise now
All unkept.
Afterwards, keep the tongue in check
Or service the other's cheek, feast,
Cup him, count pores, comb the chest,
Break him down to molecules
If you must,
While love clouds and floats above the bed
Making rain.

360°

He had stood up: I felt it rather than saw it, for I was turning over the pages of a magazine. He was behind me; my whole back was watching him.
Colette - The Captive

Reduced to straining my senses
In order to catch you somewhere in space,
The bedroom stretching behind me like a void;
I recount every significant detail of you
While hoping you are voting every inch of me
Into the lovers' hall of infamy. Casually reading I see nothing,
The words could be Dutch or Spanish like the part of you
I savored when you whispered foreign filth
In my ear. Callous morning has sabotaged us
With her mundane plans; the job, the supermarket stop,
The well-rehearsed excuse, wiping spilt tears of first children.
And your aura warming the face in my back
Will cool and I will ache a bit,
The cold creeping back into hollows
That my husband's sterile kiss will not shift.
Another week then, until bruises are calmed,
Balm smoothed skillfully into joints,
Poultices applied to shaded parts.
Then dressing, as if for a funeral
And my latest attempt to locate you in the light.

THE LOVER LEAVES THE BEDROOM NEVER TO RETURN

A toot of horns warn, his rage defies notation
And you lay, sob muffled by bend in elbow,
Listening, straining, while he unstrings you.
The duet is over, with a plosive splutter the bodies stop.
Your virtuoso solo he has taken
And spun around the room rubato.

Low, he finds his shoes, accents the laces,
The crescendo played with flair on zipper and buttons
Has brought out the best in this chamber piece.
Now though, for that aching affannoso
In the surge of strings you recognise
The inevitable lurch towards the coda.

His love ran the gamut from A to B;
You mistook a sonata for a symphony
And in a minute, after he has lowered the baton,
Exhaustion will amplify what's left of you.
Resounding, elegiac.

FALLOW

I have worried these bones for the last time,
Vertebrae chop acting as bit,
I drop what's left into the pit,
Mull over the ragged hole;
Perhaps the mass grave is to blame,
All my lovers lie as one,
Failure spread amongst the bones
As bright as battle honours.

Ash would fold in better;
Light my peat heart and torch the remains;
Lay down fallow and wait and wait,
Splintered splinters folded into the clay
Will soon render me fruitful.
And when the bed seethes,
Someone will farm me,
Sew an unexpected but persistent crop
That takes a fancy to the ground
Fights his way slowly into what has been ploughed.

AT CORE

For Lesley Blaker

The hottest day since 1911
And overhead the strip lights blur,
The gurney and the lino squeak as one
And on the table you are truly alone.

But you have prepared Matryoshka,
Shedding selves equidistant
(And us with them)
Until only the walnut knot of self remains
As concentrated as a full stop.

And in that knot is pungent fact,
Babies mothballed, linings stripped
And in a pristine guest-room womb
Hand soap slivers remain unwrapped
Along with untold possibilities.

Now the cells mutate, tumours pulse
And ghosts graft themselves into shadows.
The knife's expulsion marks the start,
The wound a doorway to perpetual doubt,
The struggle against Time's Arrow.

So much for the battle of the narrow bed.
We will you, pick yours up and walk,
The bandages shed, like reasons pulled off
And flung in the face of an absent God.

THE FALLING MAN

Has not landed yet.
His limbs are still questioning the sky
Thirty floors on.
                    Clothes rent by velocity,
Skin a flag flying the face,
Voice sandpapered away
And the sound, the sound
The roar before the body breaks.

Accelerating into oblivion,
Human debris raining all around
He makes a beautiful mark on the sky.
Nothing can catch him now,
Wind whistling through the brain
Chasing all coherent thought away,
Everything he's ever lost or found
Is compacted
                    Filed in mid-air eternity:
Rushing up as he rushes down
To fold like paper into the ground.

EMPTIES: FOUND ITEMS- AN ISLINGTON ROMANCE

A weird place for a palm tree you think. No exotic location. You can say no to a "warm" boy, but a cool boy is a much bigger catch. And what he asks of you, you give him. On Saturday night, when the parents think you are safe and sound; but here you are, girl let loose, in the dangerous moment. You didn't much want the vodka, in ten minutes the glow will be gone, but in your pockets you finger the Skittles. So now he has you lying under a concrete ledge, on top of black bags full of leaf mulch, rotting down beneath you. You wonder about your mate, is she lying with her boy somewhere similar? A concrete outhouse, the park, knickers down in a piss filled lift?

And you watch your breath crystalize over his shoulder.

There seemed to be light before, during the seduction, but as the bedroom lights in the flats go out, you are left in the pitch of intent. The dry mount, the stifled pain; you let him have you, some other time will be better than this – you'll like him still and will like him when he messes with your mind repeatedly. He doesn't tie the condom up and you can't say why, but you think he should, and when he tucks himself in, he turns, so his face is lost to you, quarter lit and you don't know why but the shame spreads over you again. When you've put yourself back together, fur hood up, frozen hands in pockets, he pulls you to your feet, before you leave, you open the Skittles, but he's not having those.

And somewhere in another corner of North London, a Mother cries in her sleep, "Not there, not there! Not with my baby!"

CORPORATION ROSES

Hybrids planted at the back of flats
In what passes for a park,
They seem to go from tight promise
To fully blown, petals ragged and unscented
Ultimately no one wants those.
One rose for each girl, similarly spent,
Blush gone at fourteen,
When those tricks born out of love
Became currency,
Spent on tower block intimacy
In a black market local economy.
No good, for all they cried out.
The boys shook the dew off the stems
And the girls thickened into mothers,
Into their mothers,
Into what has always been.

TOBACCO NESTS

The barren forest of a dozen poplars
Wave, but do not curse at February.
Under the weight of a derelict sky,
Tobacco nests lodged in boughs
Stand firm against what's left of winter.
It says much for the crow engineers
And the sapless strength of these windbreakers,
Suffering from seasonal osteoporosis.
Still the bowls clean of black down cling,
Air empty of raucous chav chatter.

The earth has taken sleeping pills.
Will emerge groggy with doubt,
Appear as cathartic cloudbursts,
Pushing shoots, promising a murder of crows.

PELLET

It's Squeak alright.

My Persil mouse has paid dearly for his liberation
Achieved after many hours of secret gnawing –
And him so friendly with his jailer. A perfect pellet,
Nutrients stripped from the fur-lined skeletal crush,
A rainbow membrane embraces bones, a pelt of sudden showers.
"Naawww", Dad rolls the remains in ingrained hands,
"Didn't stand much of a chance against the Vicarage owl"
I think of last night's moon and cringe,
Wingspan shrouding the ground, talons tearing in -
The image swims. Laid out on the bunker we wrap him tenderly,
Cartoons enfold his little body, double mummified now.
We look for a moment right along the food chain, a far distant kink
The moment Cro-Magnon man got a grip and we ascended.
Then in with the roses, a carbon cousin, went my mouse.